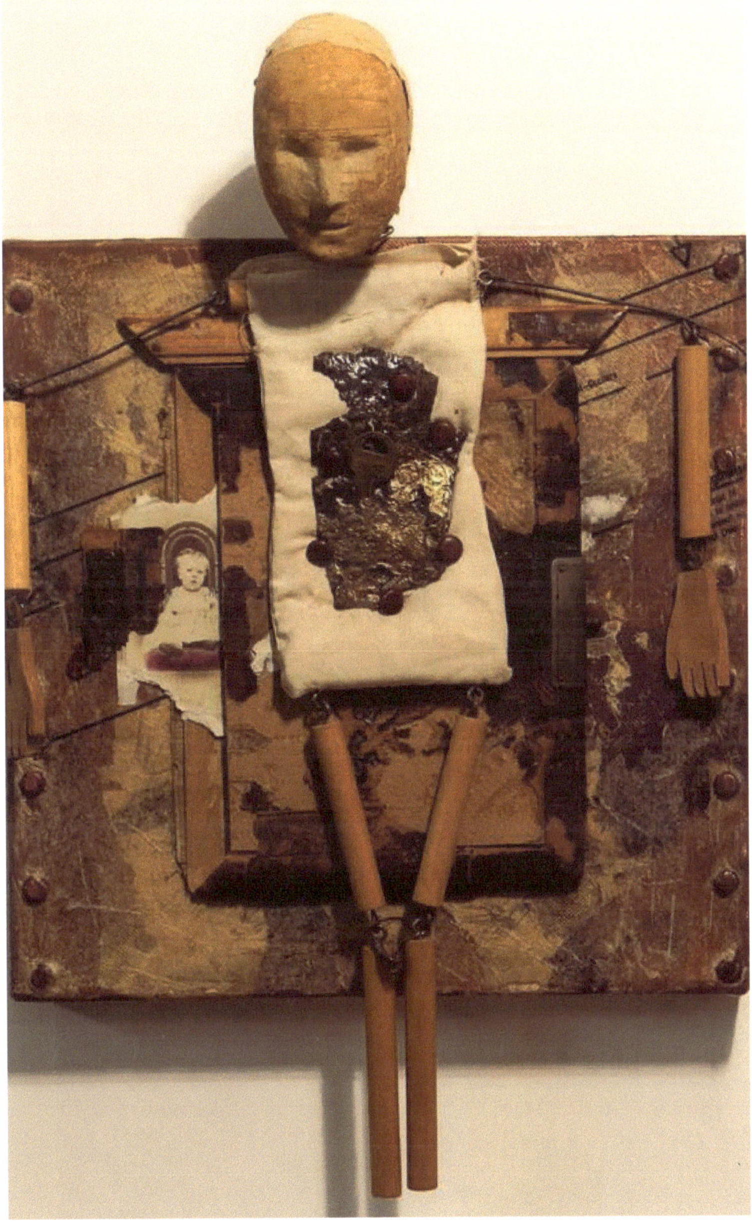

Circus of the Unconscious Mind

text by

images by

Hoyt Hilsman

Nancy Kay Turner

The love we bear for bread is an outstanding choice in the waiver between relationships and artichokes.

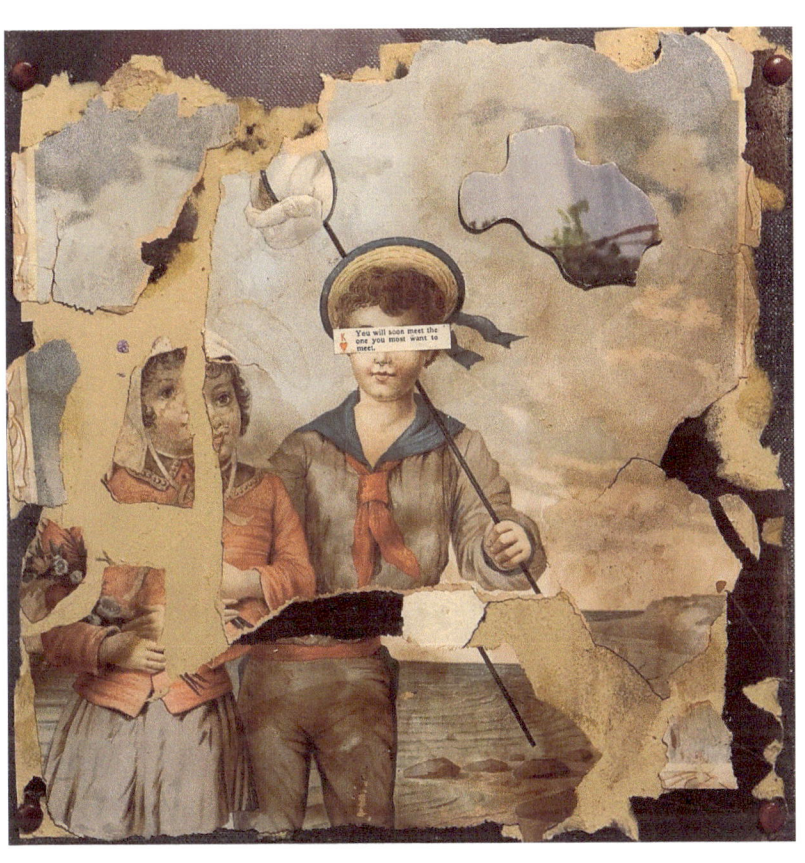

I went over to their trailer where a blaze of light shot up at the infinite goo. Where it was going I wasn't sure, but after a couple of hours the toast was burned. I was finally shocked and pregnant over the whole delicatessen.

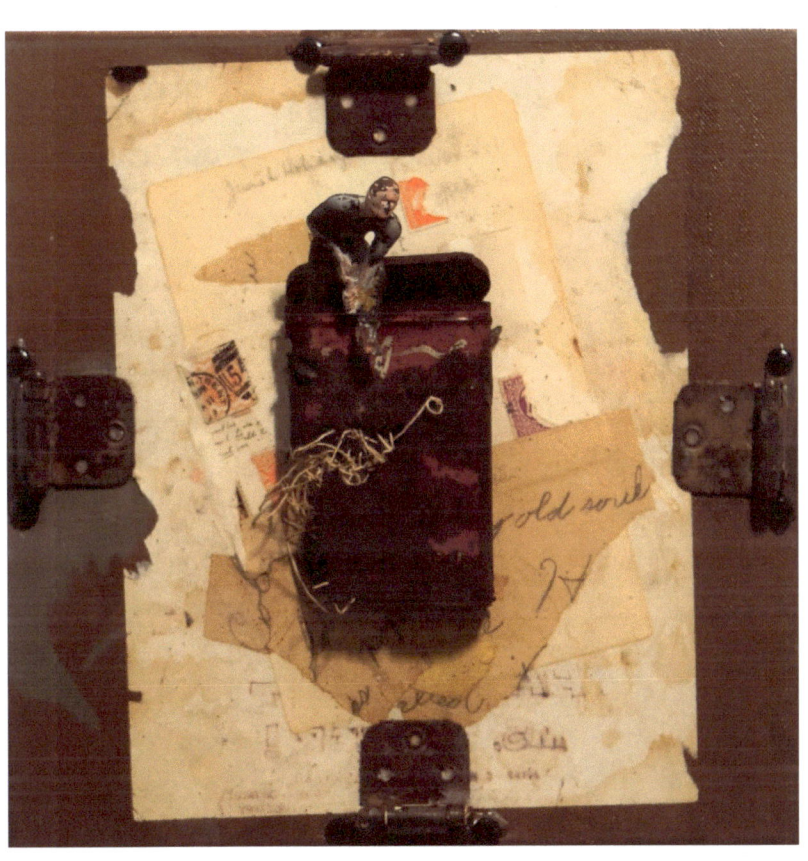

Frightful ideas wrought from pickles and other gargantuan blimps show up for dinner.

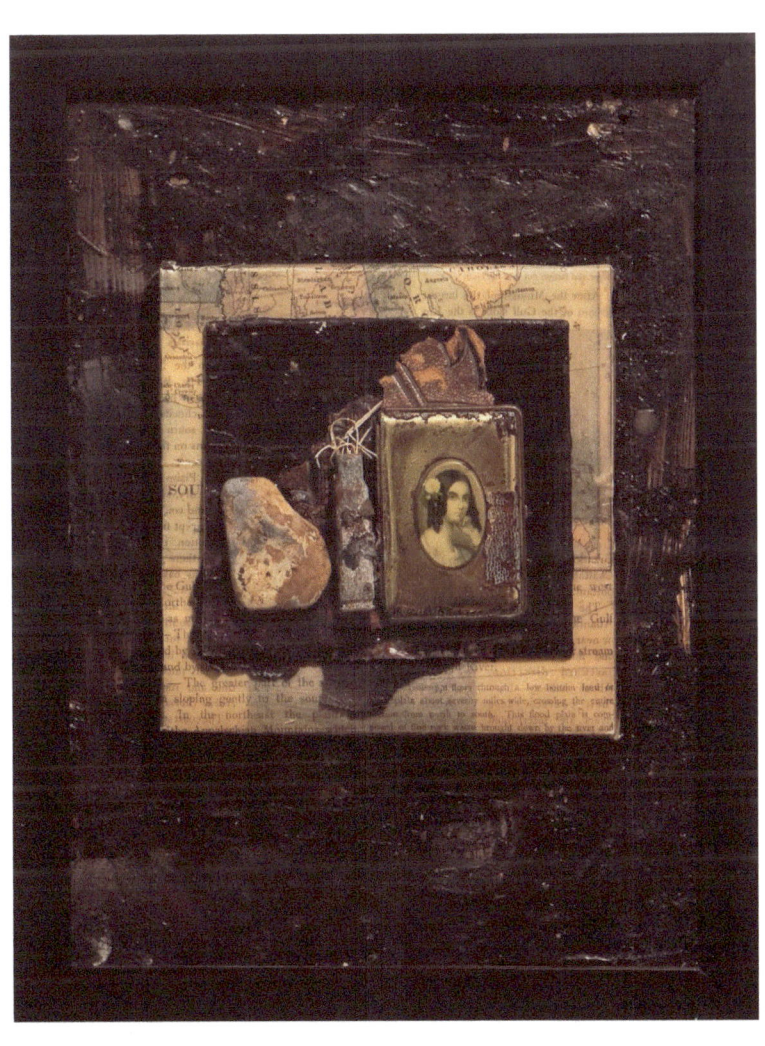

If you could follow what I was saying, your red wagon would probably fall over a cliff and you would fly up to the tallest beacon in the cave.

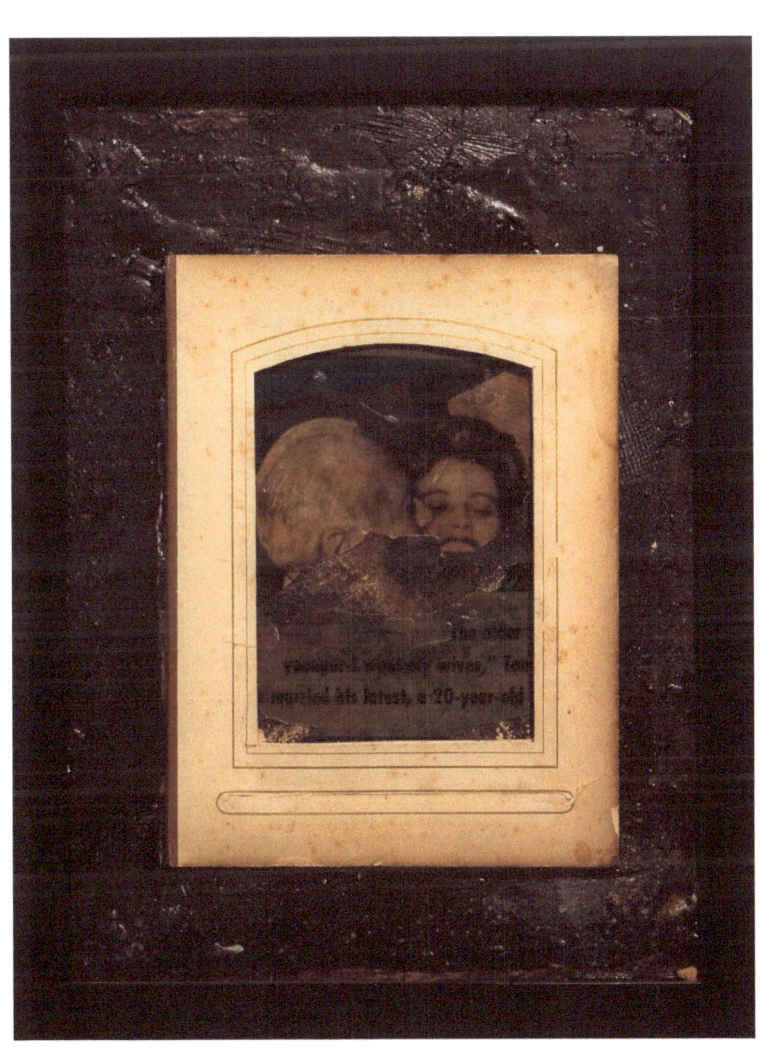

I know that I could communicate with you across time and forever, but the glasses were flying into peanut butter and I stopped feeling anything. Except late at night when I slid for the toothbrush stand and we made mercy when the stars were brightly fogged.

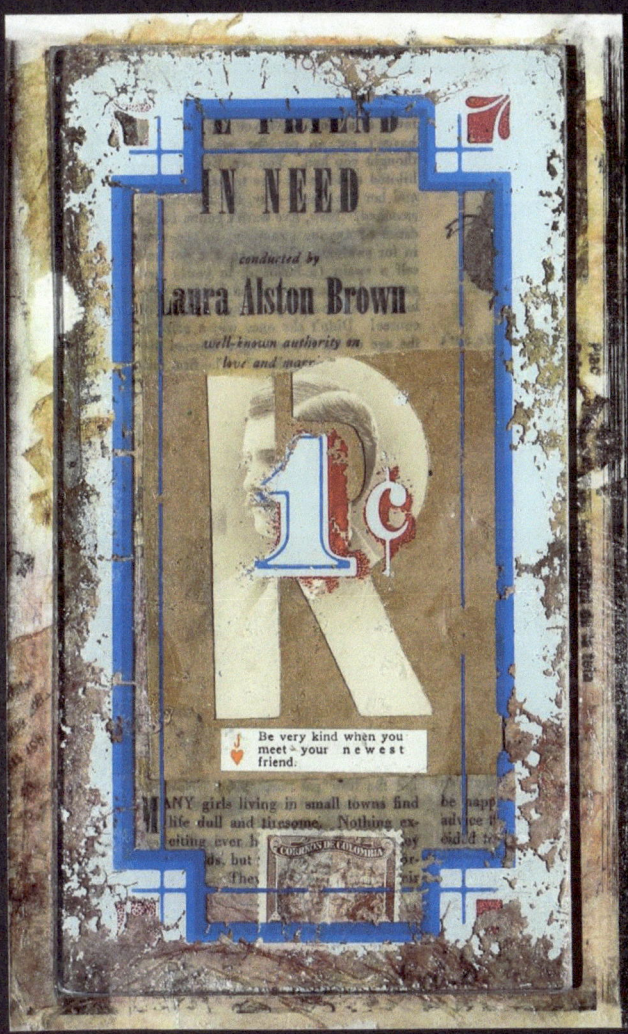

Checkerboard squares is a place that I used to go during Sunday night TV and it almost cost me my whole baseball card collection until Miller Young called one of the kids "Jew" on the playground and the D.A.R. was making a special trip to see Bozo the Clown.

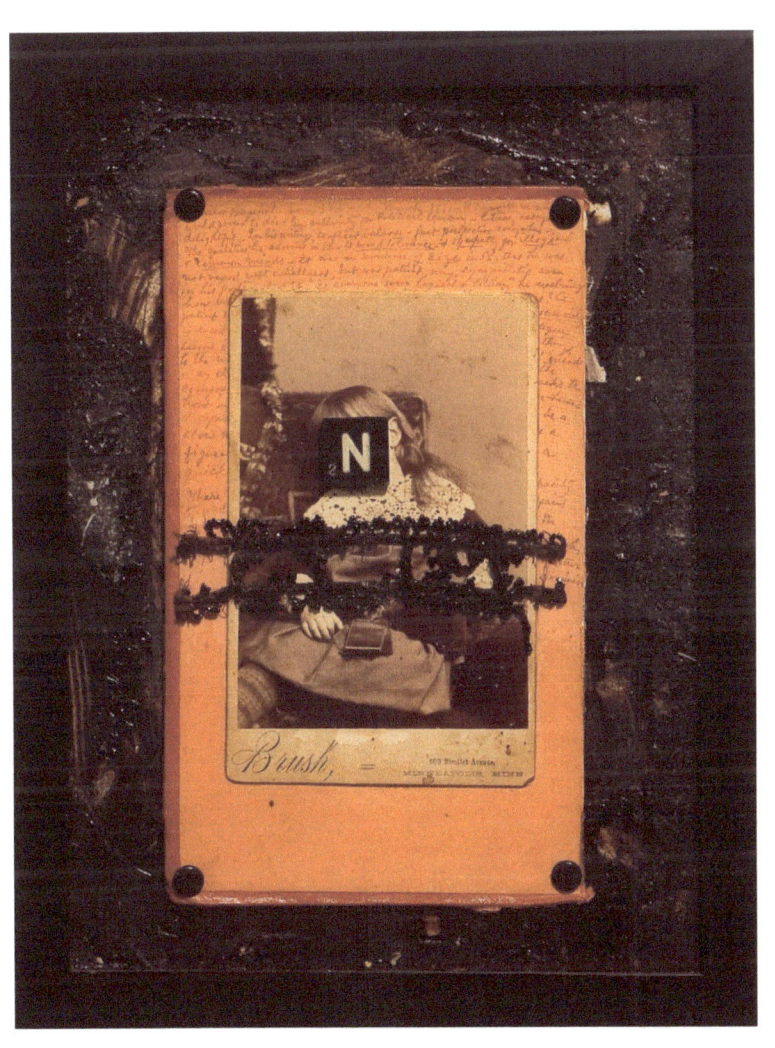

Motivation let me signal for distress until I was nearly out of aerosol. I went looking for matches almost suddenly but the flavor lost something in translation.

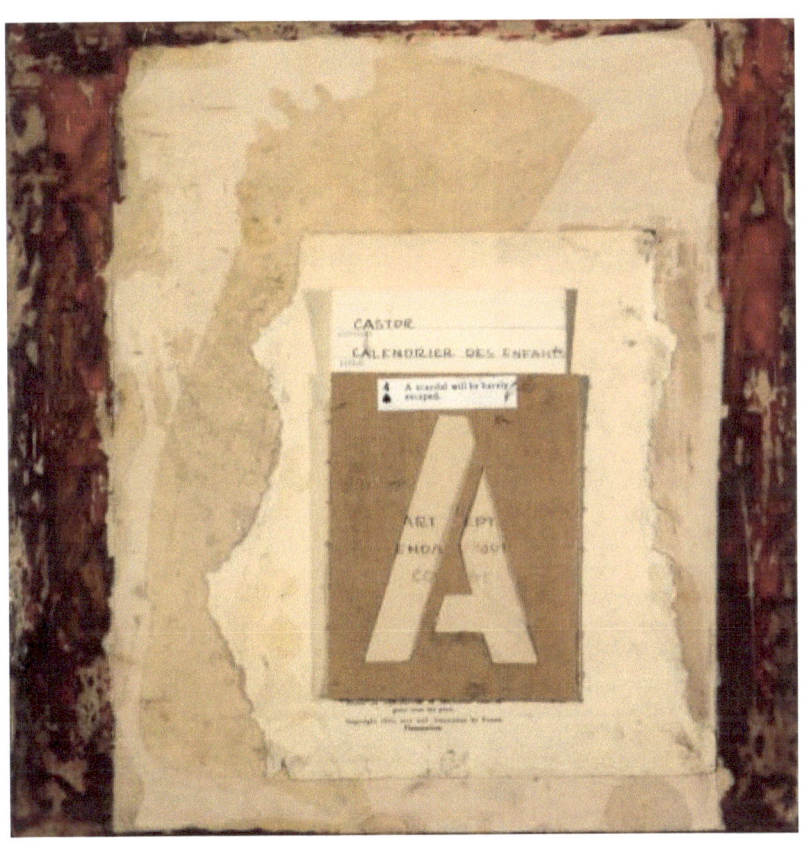

Watching out for busboys and the stress of complaints whenever the stars play bingo, it was lost on me how much waste was intended for City Hall parking structures in the dismal slackery that I repaired to suspend.

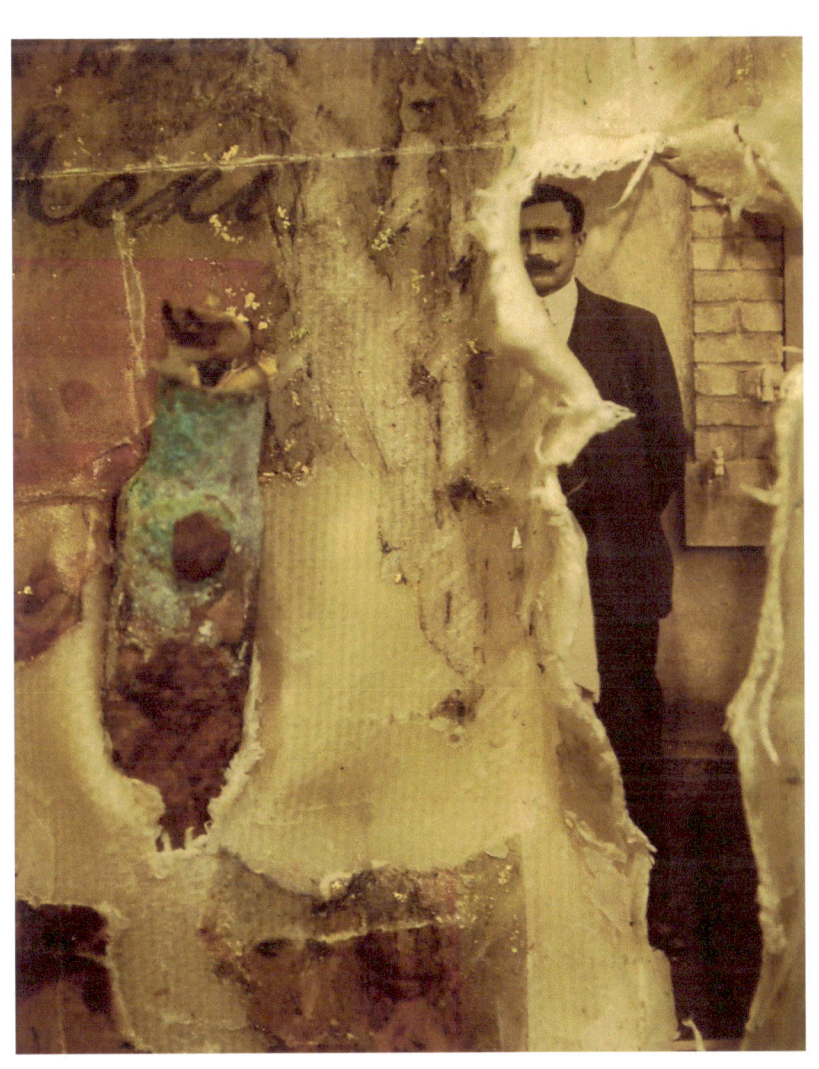

If you were incognito I would forget all about the quackery on your head. But it became almost truthful when she flew past like a wagon. I was concretely puzzled and blasted back like a simmering plot.

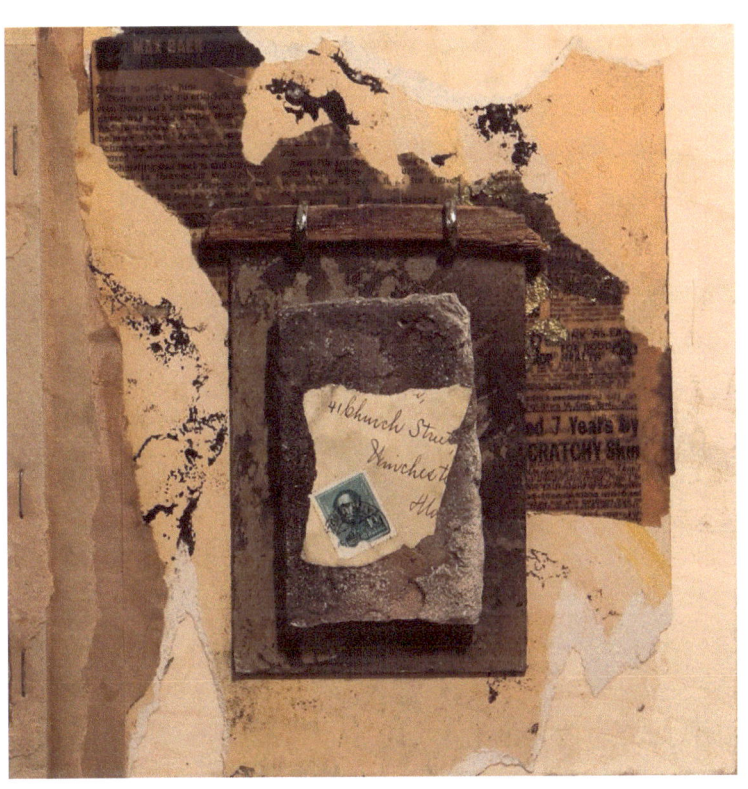

I am actually writing poetry, which is a conviction that potatoes would not suit Rhoda, especially since he hurried past her, rushing for the brain trust. It was with profound regret that Shelly did that again. We can only hope that cooler brains replace the peat bog, or that once in a sparrow there will be greater understanding and file gumbo.

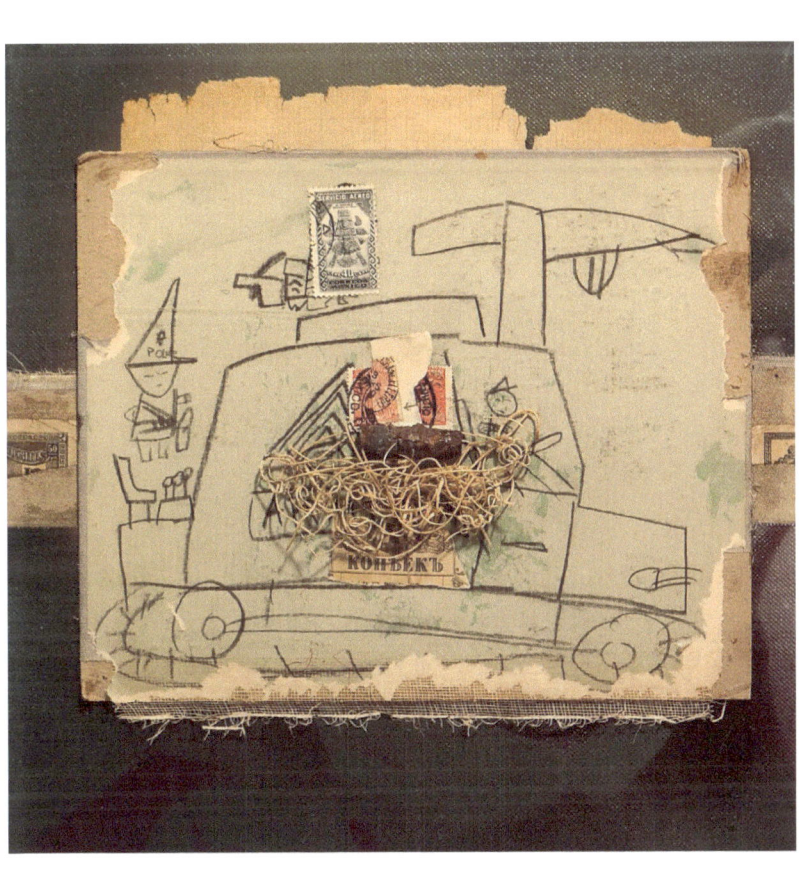

I idolized Sambo under the bark until it got hotter than Perseus. Whoever calls up at dinnertime when it could also be raining upstairs until the cat comes down for breakfast?

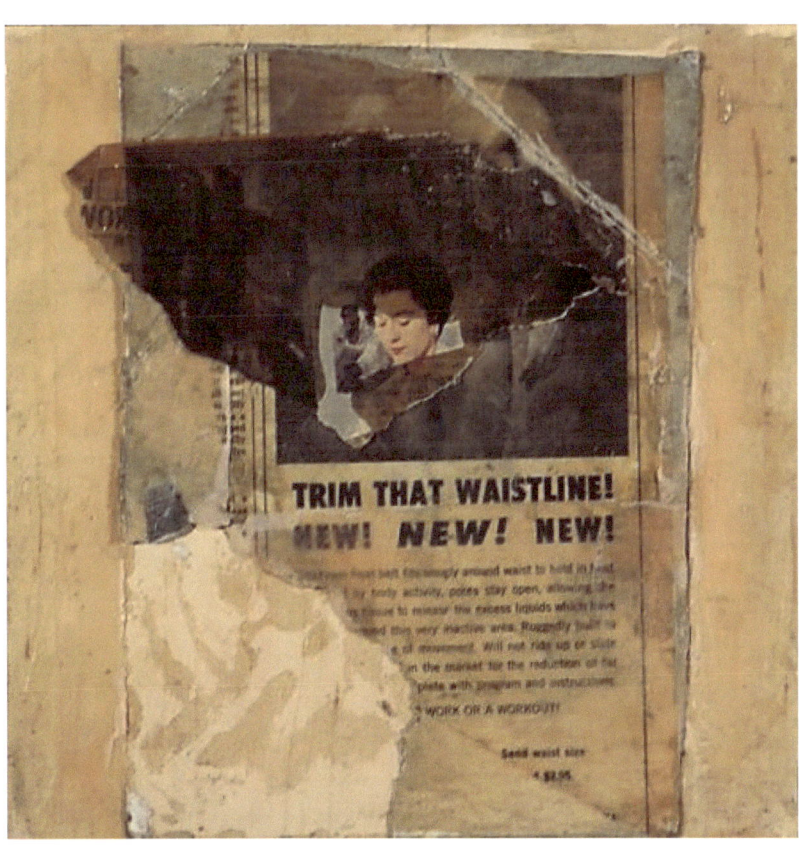

Something stroked him and he couldn't speak for crazy fruit. It made me fetid and unsure. What is cantaloupe do not exist? Is there an answer in that bale of hay? My sleepless carpool was stuck by incessant schools of trout, grappling with each fraction while trying to steer into the passageway where the conference was being held.

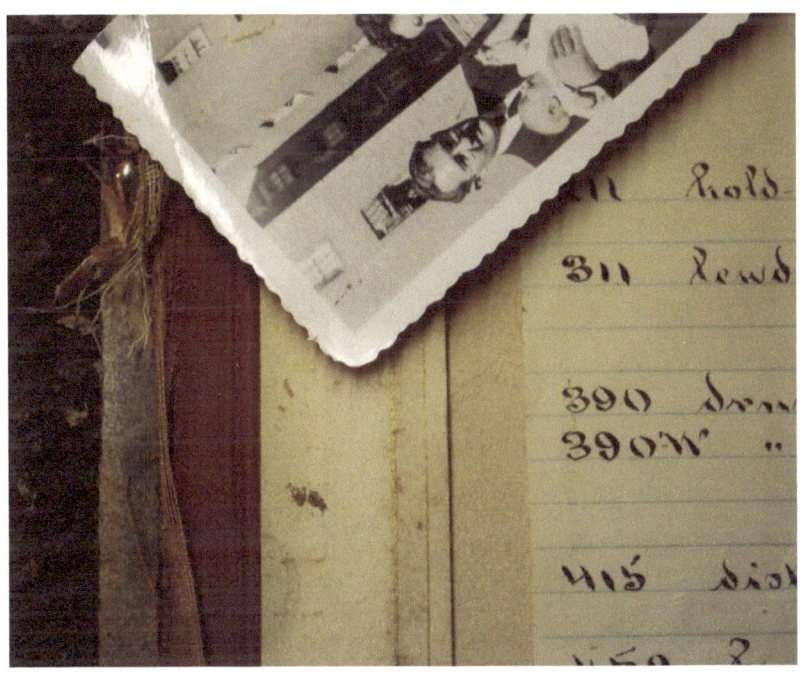

311 hold—

311 lewd

390 dem

390W "

415 dic

459 3.

"You are spiritual person," she toasted until it was awful. There must be some truth in the sky or an impossible wording where the hole used to be before it was filled up with vermiculite. I would be sorry if they sent it all back to Mary Kay without the least goodbye strain of grapefruit juice.

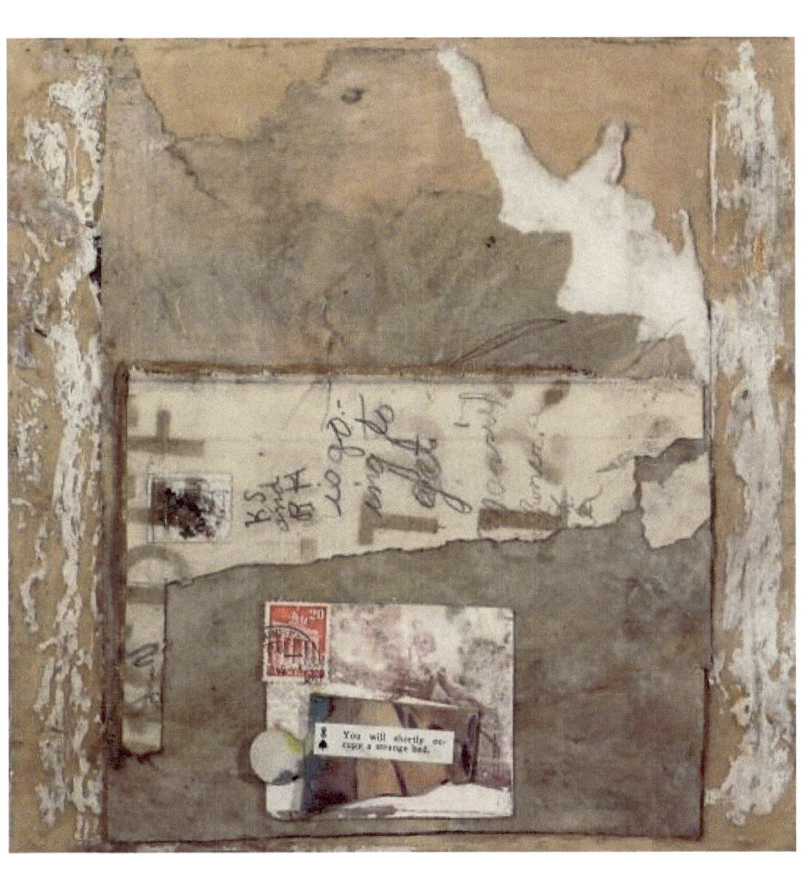

"Chupacabras," they answered with a gleeful trance. Not once did I try to cry. It was hard but tasty. I was ungone outside into the drizzle when I heard them call back with a photo album and streaks of cotton. My heart was riddled.

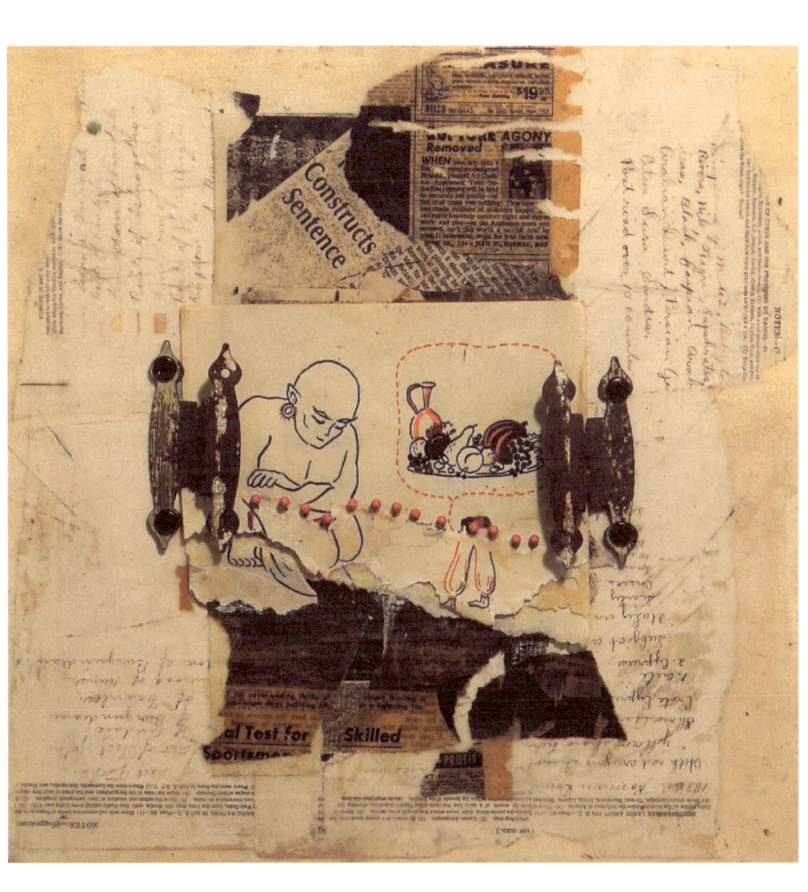

He heard what I was saying but chose to jaywalk into the baseball diamond up above. It represented tranquility and a state of circus where the humiliation played around in the bullrushes. I almost forgot everything.

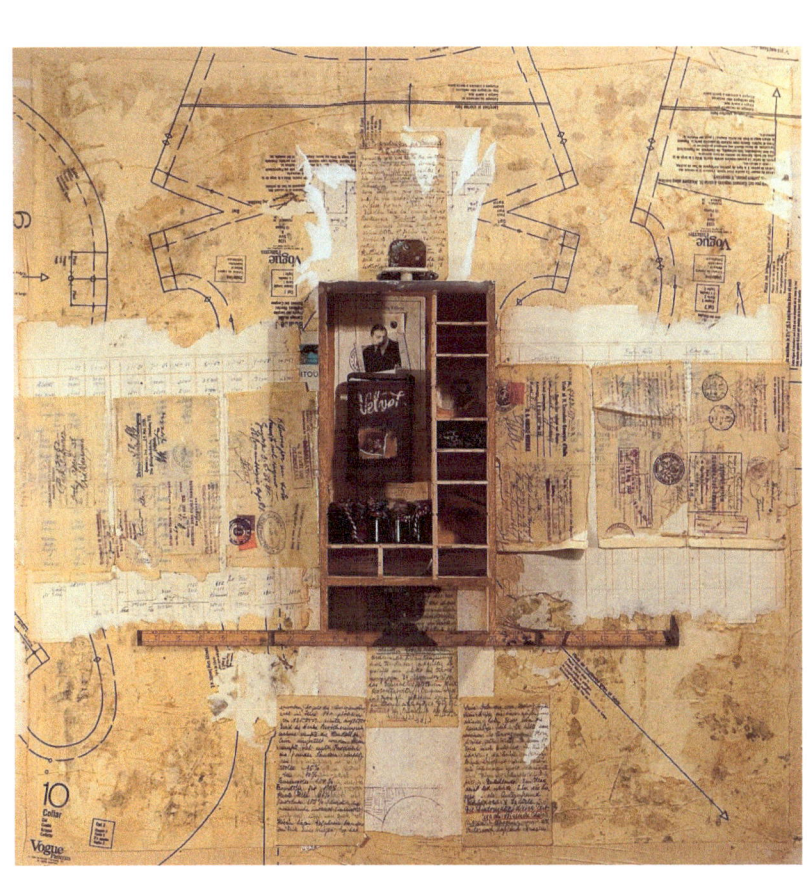

Maximum coffee words appease some people. Her grandmother talked about hysterectomies but "little pitchers" wander around in circles dreaming of breasts and dodge ball. It could have worked out okay, but was Ohio standing over him relating to the underbrush and singing about Time magazine or maybe TV Guide.

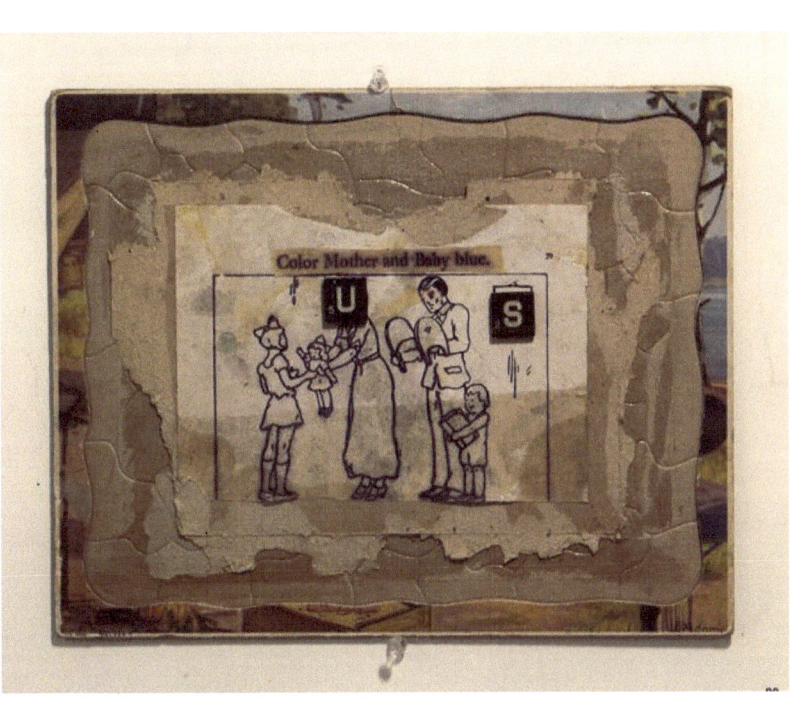

"Dive in or be pigged in the process," was the motto for the regiment of idiotic carpenters when their expressed their deepest emotion for the airline crew. It was a respectful occasion and dairy foods were passed out on the floorboards.

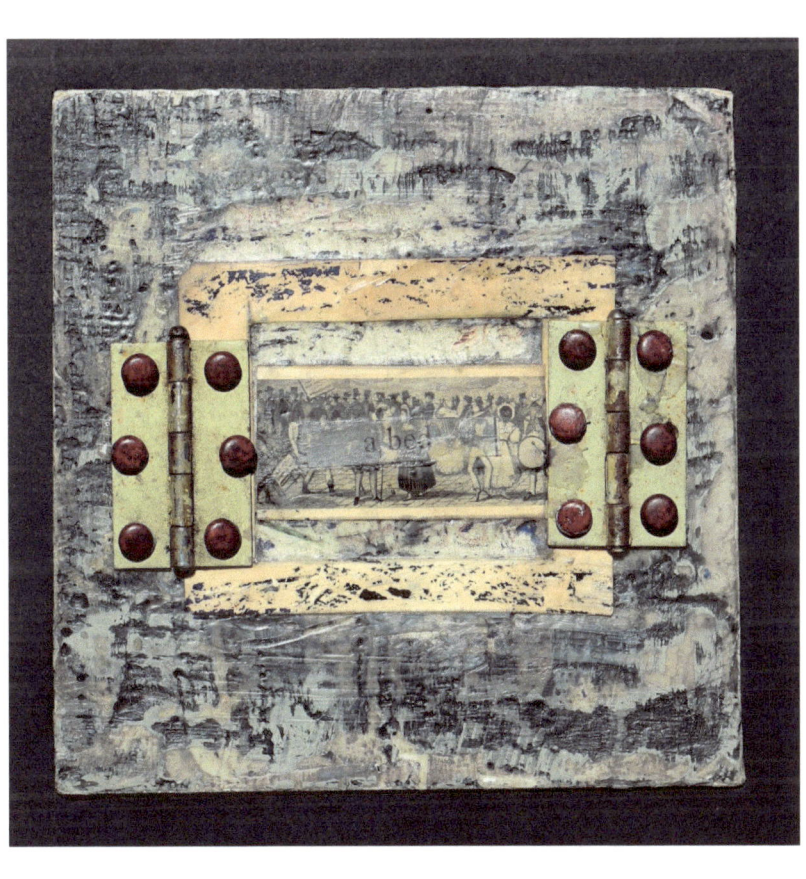

Rapid ringlets were my preference, but I didn't have much to countenance in the dimmed light of schoolyards and bullpens. What struck me sideways was the relenting forays of mongooses that paddled in circles about the den mother. It wouldn't have taken very long to get the picture, but I subsided.

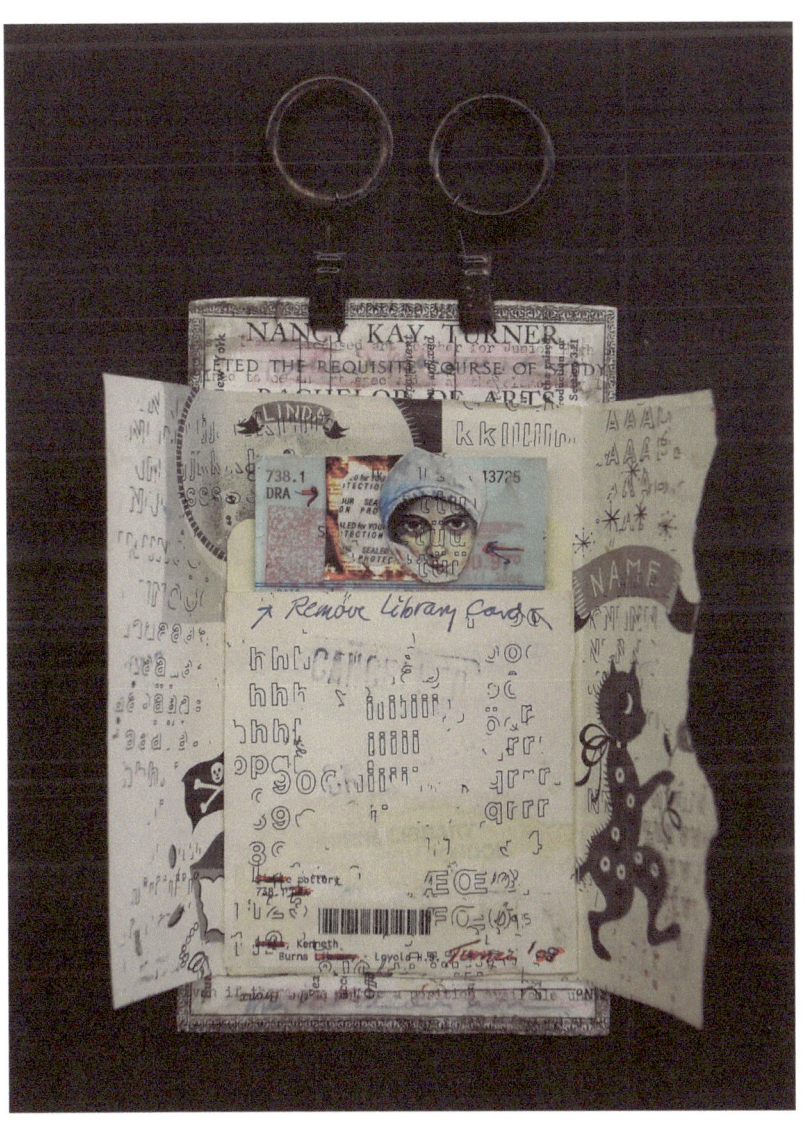

She made plans under the timetable at Fury Station, where nobody watched except a squirrel from across Arden Road who wondered why the interplanetary travel drew poor notices for Alpha males except during the monsoon season.

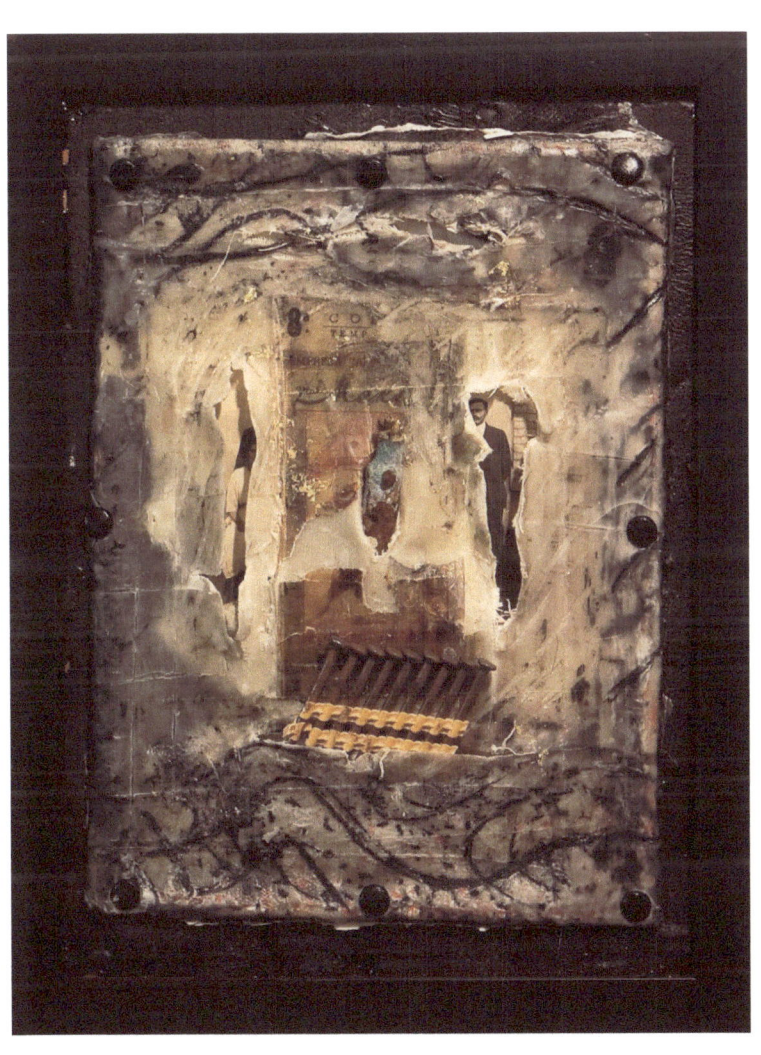

It would blend out the membranes if I tried to forgive her debutante beside everything else. It was enough machination to digest most purity in disguise or rebel against anything else except the sky warfare. I was earnestly baffled when it was all arranged without fracas and dispensed in small tubes at the bottom of sea worms.

Rubbing Her The Wrong Way

Along with the 15 dream texts 21 mixed media drawings are on

RUBBING HER THE WRONG WAY

pictures or icons. /// Two and perhaps more importantly, they

RuBBinG HeR ThE WrONg WaY

drawings therefore may rema
t seperate entities or may become one whole piece. This docum
ent because each drawing has not only the picture but the one
word of the title within the picture title. Does this word
title the drawing? Does it only have significance as it fit
into its proper sequence in the full title? Or is it a word
with no specific value? These are all possibilities which co
could read are ...

Rubbing Her The Wrong Way

This rela...
ry might be...   As one looks into

RUBBING HER THE WRONG WAY

1,   raised

RuBBinG HeR ThE WrONg WaY

is questioned is the
word   within the picture then
becomes   relationship of one image to the
other boo...   haunting and dreamlike. The i...
unequiv...   get ... wed into a state of mind or mo   a fetch it
As one enters ...   the picture Southern for
example on...   ons between cacti and alligators
set in egy...pt ...   landscapes

Empty lands...   setting for different kinds of
interactio...   between cacti and alligators
the cac...   like looming monumental
structure...   the desert heat casting long shadows
across the sand...   semi-religious. The alligators
look ///   ...tures look animated and whimsical
seemingly...   LA   to LAS VEGAS

The earl...   some settings for more
tropical places...   paradises with large citys
on the horizon ...   looking like posted guards
allowing ...   ...es to enter. Interplaying
within the ...   ...land sections of sky showing
differently ...   ...et.

NO.

Another B

www.ingramcontent.com/pod-product-compliance
Lightning Source LLC
Chambersburg PA
CBHW040818200526
45159CB00024B/3024